BLOSSOMING
THROUGH VIRTUES

ARLES BALLESTEROS

BLOSSOMING
THROUGH VIRTUES

STORIES, TECHNIQUES, AND REFLECTIONS
THAT WILL HELP YOU ACHIEVE A BETTER
QUALITY OF LIFE

Quisqueyana Press
San Diego, California, USA

Blossoming Through Virtues

Stories, techniques, and reflections that will help
you achieve a better quality of life
By: Arles Ballesteros

Copyright© 2022 Arles Ballesteros

ISBN: 979-8-9855858-7-2 (Paperback English version)

Library of Congress Control Number: 2022908742

See other versions:

ISBN: 979-8-8472592-2-4 Hardcover (Spanish version)
ISBN: 979-8-8472533-7-6 Hardcover (English version)
ISBN: 979-8-9855858-5-8 Paperback (Spanish version)
eBook ASIN: B0BB4H3VHD (English version)
eBook ASIN: B0BB5D19SB (Spanish version)

To order additional copies of the book, visit
www.quisqueyanapress.com/store, amazon.com or contact:

QUISQUEYANA
Press

Quisqueyana Press
Poway, California, USA
info@quisqueyanapress.com
www.quisqueyanapress.com

"... naked, and ye clothed Me; I was sick, and ye visited Me; I was in prison, and ye came unto Me."

Matthew 25:86 KJ21

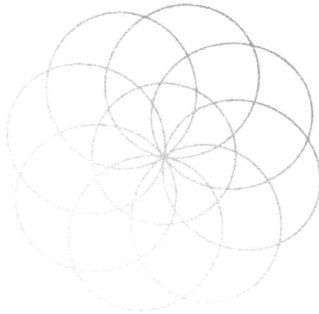

DEDICATION

I dedicate this book, "Blossoming Through Virtues," to all my friends. Especially seafarers who leave their homes and go to the seas of remote countries aboard cruise ships, not for pleasure but as the only alternative to support their families. To my former fellow waiters with whom I shared the same experiences in several hotels in the port city of La Ceiba in my country of origin, Honduras.

To my colleagues and staff at the Monteleone Hotel in New Orleans, USA.

I dedicate it to my talented barber friends. While they were grooming me by cutting my hair, they encouraged me so that my dream of writing this book would become a reality today. They are Javier, Duval, Juan, and Elmer.

I dedicate it to millions of human beings. To the couples and families who seek to develop their nobility and qualities. And the people who enjoy helping others, instead of thinking only about money. To those who long to learn to live and enjoy the joys that God gives us throughout our existence.

ACKNOWLEDGMENTS

The year 2017 saw the laying of the first cornerstone of this book, which is entitled Blossoming Through Virtues, when I began my first analysis of people with prodigious virtues.

This work reflects the knowledge and concepts acquired after reading several sapiential books found in the Bible.

In addition, I have had the help of genuinely extraordinary people, such as Robert T. Kiyosaki, Napoleon Hill, Sergio Fernández, and Raimon Samsó. These men, through their works, have inspired me to help others.

I thank the Divine Creator of the universe for having enlightened my life with a beautiful family and the beautiful gifts and charisma he gave me.

I am entirely grateful to my wife, Ana, for her advice, patience, and help in developing the first draft of the manuscript.

I thank my daughter Yorkel for her excellent participation in the final revision of this book.

Likewise, I thank my daughter Melsy for her support in introducing me to the world of computers. In the same way, I give a special thanks to María Aduke Alabi for her collaboration in making possible the edition of this work that you hold in your hands.

And finally, I thank you for making the wise decision to gain the book that I have written with much will and love.

Arles Ballesteros, New Orleans

INDEX

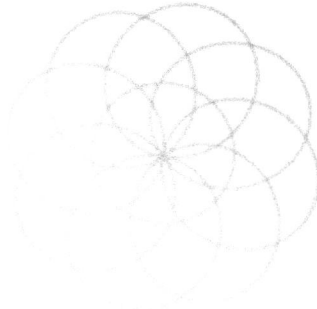

FOREWORD

His deep desire to give the world a book that reconstructs lives is justified.

Arles Ballesteros is a self-taught writer born in Olanchito, Honduras's civic city. It is the cradle and heaven of renowned authors, among them Ramón Amaya Amador, author of the book Green Prison (Prisión Verde).

In gratitude for the grace received, he puts his great work called Blossoming Through Virtues in your hands.

This book contains nineteen chapters and gathers in their writings that generate growth and positive thoughts that simultaneously sensitize your existence, directing it with love towards the common good.

For example, on pages 115 and 153, you will find the texts entitled.

1. I'm Sick of Life (Estoy harto de la vida.)
2. The Little Angels (Los angelitos.)

These are two integrative reflections in which social differences are annulled and help you recognize your real inclusion in every moment of life, whether alone or in the company.

Adding your presence to this book will open your mind to find the intuitive solution to internal or external conflicts and, at the same time, fill your emptiness. Then, we will have succeeded in this great work that has been made for you with love and much passion.

Ana de Ballesteros

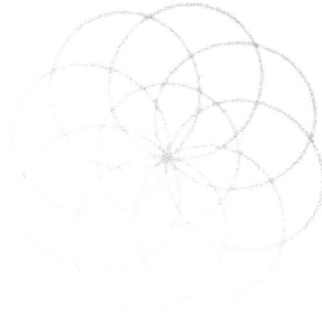

INTRODUCTION

The virtues are man's moral heritage; they help him behave well in all circumstances.

Human blossoming is a value that places people at the center of all their activities and initiatives.

Among some of these virtues are gratitude, forbearance, and honesty, but there are two that are the most important:

1. Humility is the mother of all other virtues since it leads us to accept our defects, weaknesses, and limitations.

2. Courage, or bravery, is always needed to tell the truth, remain cheerful and optimistic amid the most challenging moments, and forgive when a wound still hurts. Any virtue you want to cultivate will demand courage.

The practice of virtues allows us to acquire true wisdom. It helps us become better people and avoid living superficial lives, which are guided only by the pursuit of material wealth and status.

Through this book, I share stories, techniques, and reflections that will help you find and live a more blossoming life.

For example, you could discover a new skill and create a new way of sharing time, talents, and even money, improving many human beings' lives.

You will develop the will to cultivate an increasingly healthy and good soul, love and enjoy the surrounding people, be generous with your things, and gain many friends.

People like the learning process through listening or reading stories, so I decided to use this way as an essential tool to bring you this message about human welfare.

Through this piece, I will share some of my ways of helping others with you.

Now, without further ado, let's enjoy this writing.

THE
VIRTUES

ONE

AFFABILITY

It can be associated with kindness, courtesy, and friendliness. When a person is affable, he/she shows simplicity, sympathy, frankness, and empathy in his/her social relations.

When receiving a visitor, an affable person is attentive, offering something to drink or trying to make the visitor feel comfortable.

The opposite of affability is antipathy or rudeness.

In this case, people have a harsh and cold behavior.

In addition, we could establish that when a person wishes to improve the level of agreeableness, he/she should take the following steps:

- He/she should strive to be more careful in his dealings with others.
- Every wise person should have the gift of kindness, making life much more pleasant for all those with whom he/she lives.

Affability is related to fairness since both allow any human being to behave in the best possible way with others.

Grumpiness, rudeness, and discourtesy are the opposite of being polite. A polite greeting or a kind comment can brighten a person's day.

For example, one man can politely ask his neighbor to turn down the music without being aggressive or violent and disturbing the peaceful coexistence. Another, on the other hand, can get into a senseless argument because of his lack of affability.

Affability is an essential virtue for a healthy human coexistence.

Treating others with gentleness manifests a genuine spirit of love that contributes to the blossoming of people.

KINDNESS BEGINS AT HOME

I will share with you a fragment of my life.

When I was a nine-year-old boy, I lived with my parents and siblings on a "Palo Verde" banana farm in "Coyoles." It was the center of all the banana farms in the municipality of "Olanchito," department of Yoro, in Honduras.

These banana crops belonged to the transnational Standard Fruit Company, founded in the United States in 1924 by the Vaccaro brothers. Their way of operating was that they stowed the bananas in freight cars. They were transported by railroad to the port of La Ceiba and placed inside a cargo ship that later transported them by sea to the city of New Orleans in the US. Sometimes, the product was sent to the Asian continent and Europe.

Our home comprised a family of eleven members: my parents and my three sisters; Norma is the eldest, then Araceli, and Marieta, who at that time had become emancipated, and six brothers, from oldest to youngest: Wilfredo, Felipe, Hector, Arles, Richard, and Sergio.

My devoted mother, Anastasia, fomented love in the home naturally. One of her methods was to encourage us to exchange clothes. Especially during the winter, when it was difficult to wash clothes because we had no washing machine or dryer. The barracks where we lived were not provided with electricity.

When my sisters or mother, who cooked and washed our clothes, were absent, we distributed the household chores among all the siblings. Some would prepare the food for a while, while others would go into the dense banana farms to take breakfast or lunch to my father at the place where he was working.

My dear reader, the point I am eager to share with you is the particular case of one of my family members.

Richard was one of my brothers, two years younger than me. At one year and ten months, he accidentally ingested kerosene gas. And, perhaps because of my parents' ignorance, the case was not followed up medically.

As time went on, the poison progressively damaged his brain to a point where it caused epileptic seizures, neurocognitive disorders, and mixed dependency.

Richard, at seven years old, was dependent. His health condition demanded the care of a one-year-old child, so, with much love, all of us siblings, without exception, groomed him, dressed him, served him his meals, and assisted him when he went to sleep. Besides this, since we did not have a wheelchair, this servant would mount him on a one-wheeled handcrafted cart three times a week and take him for a ride around the block. Back then, I came to experience a lot of compassion for my little brother Richard when living that experience. Especially when he was just a seven-year-old boy, he suffered epileptic seizures.

Sometimes I think God brought him into this world as a means for us to learn to give true love to our fellow man.

Dear reader, thank you for letting me confess that while I was writing this paragraph about Richard's life, I couldn't avoid crying and shed many tears. Many of us do not value the health that God gives his children. I invite you to thank God for your life, health, family, and blessings that you receive from above when you get up from your bed in the morning.

As time went by, we grew and migrated, looking for ways to foster our blossoming.

Norma is currently a micro-entrepreneur and owner of a restaurant.

Wilfredo is today an excellent tailor. He told me an anecdote I would like to share. He met a friend in New Orleans on a particular occasion he had not seen for a long time. While they were talking, my brother noticed the man was fidgeting every time he tried to sit down. Wilfredo asked him what was wrong, and the man answered that he had hemorrhoids. Wilfredo immediately took him to the hospital emergency room, where he underwent surgery. Thanks to my brother's role as a good Samaritan, he miraculously saved his life.

Felipe is currently a "retired" lieutenant of infantry and is also a writer, author of the books:

1. My son and me (Mi Hijo y Yo).
2. The Lonely Men's Island (La Isla de los Hombres Solos).

3. Telaco Defying Destiny (Telaco Desafiando al Destino).

Because of his great virtue, Sergio, the youngest, is now an active officer with the rank of lieutenant colonel, whom I admire very much for his noble qualities and humility.

Richard, who accidentally ingested kerosene gas, passed on to a better life. Today, he is a little angel who enjoys the presence of God; he passed away at the age of 14.

Arles is happily married and has three daughters, a son, two granddaughters, and a grandson. He has a great inclination for art and likes to help others.

- I am a self-taught writer, author of the literary work: Blossoming Through Virtues.
- Bachelor in business administration.
- "Retired" sailor.
- An expert welder in the manufacture of residential gratings.
- An expert artisan makes sculptures using forks, knives, and tablespoons as raw material.
- Expert in the art of "origami."

- Fond of playing musical instruments: guitar, piano, and drums.

TWO

THE CHARISMA

We all can be charismatic. It is a skill you can learn. Being charitable to others is a spiritual good that allows you to see life from another person's perspective.

We have all met at least one person full of vitality which seems to make friends. People admire and appreciate them; such people prove they can achieve any goal they set their minds to, and all doors open in their path as if the world conforms to their desires.

They are successful, have good jobs, a lovely family, enormous houses, go on vacations to paradisiacal places, and, strangely enough, nobody envies them because everybody likes them.

People around charismatic individuals feel confident and secure with them; they have admiration for these individuals and find it very easy to get along with them. These people manage to bring out the best in others; giving them a sense of integration by feeling that they listen to your opinions.

Charismatic people can build positive relationships much more accessible than others, making them stand out as leaders and friendly people.

For this reason, they are often chosen to occupy the best jobs or to win people's favor.

Being generous with others is essential for our healthy coexistence as humans and our general well-being.

One of how we can be charitable is by volunteering our time, no matter how long or short it is.

Giving your quality time is being present with others to support them practically.

For example, it could be serving food at a shelter, helping during a natural disaster, volunteering to drive older people to appointments, preparing dinner for a sick neighbor, or any activity that allows you to help and get to know those around you need your help.

You may have some personal qualities you can share with others. For example, your enthusiasm, hope, gratitude, patience, and love, or you can set out to enhance these qualities or adopt them in your own life. For example, you can patiently listen to a person as they share their story of being out of work or offer encouragement to someone feeling discouraged.

THE PRACTICE OF MAGNANIMITY

Magnanimity is evident in a person who has a noble temperament and greatness of spirit. It is a disposition to give more than what is considered normal, undertake without fear, give oneself to the last consequences, and advance despite adversity.

Magnanimity is the virtue that turns a simple human being into a hero.

Some years ago, I was working onboard a cruise ship; I met a generous character named Ergin. He was the manager in charge of the "Windjammer" restaurant, located on the ship's upper deck, where we provided buffet service to the passengers.

Mr. Ergin led a group of approximately sixty people, comprising his assistants, waiters, and cooks.

Whenever Ergin moved through any restaurant area, he greeted friendly and interacted with everyone in his path. He practiced the virtue of lifting people's spirits through gentle and funny jokes.

Ergin's personality was striking and stood out from most of the crew; we enjoyed working with him because of the charisma that characterized him.

One day, we were several fellow waiters wrapping knives and forks in cloth napkins, then we would put them inside a thin wicker basket, and, once filled, we would move them to the buffet line. Suddenly, Mr. Ergin arrived and noticed that we were all serious, so he approached the shortest young man in the group and asked him: why are you so severe? Do you want to fight with me? Before the young man answered, Ergin positioned himself in his front like a boxer, but with his guard down as if ready to receive his opponent's blows.

When we saw Mr. Ergin, who was about two meters tall, in front of that young boy of one and a half meters, we all laughed. Once he achieved his goal, left satisfied for having lifted our spirits, we could not stop laughing. From that moment on, we worked with enthusiasm and joy.

I will share another brief anecdote with you about Mr. Ergin's magnanimity. One night, when it was about eight forty, I was on the ship's deck; we were sailing at sea at a speed of about twenty knots, which equals thirty-seven kilometers per hour.

I was doing the day's closing; it was moving several pool lounge chaises to the warehouse's interior. Suddenly, when I was about to take the first one in, I perceived the wind shaking the chaise in my hands; it was so strong that it endangered me to drag me to the sea. When noticing the danger, I returned the chaise to its place and asked for help at the restaurant "Windjammer." I went in and told Mr. Ergin what had happened. He replied two people should do this task and offered to help me.

He accompanied me to the ship's deck, and when we reached the place, we each took one end of the chaise and moved them until we placed them inside the hold, which was about 131 feet away.

In this way, Mr. Ergin showed me and gave me part of his nobility.

I wish every person, business people, to stop mistreating their subordinates, giving up victimizing them, to educating and guiding them properly, with kindness, as Mr. Ergin does.

His generosity characterizes Ergin, and that is why he now holds the position of senior superintendent in the most powerful cruise company in the world: Royal Caribbean International.

THREE

SELF-ESTEEM

Now, more than ever, we must value love and be grateful for the gift of life. There are thousands of people who, on this day, have ceased to exist in this world, and you are still here.

Besides, suppose we work, study, progress, or achieve goals. In that case, it is a great privilege to have a birthday celebration, to have someone to share with. We should value and appreciate it; however, this is in total contrast with all the World Health Organization's reports.

This organization says that depression and low self-esteem have increased exponentially, and suicides in young people between fifteen and twenty-nine outnumber deaths from traffic accidents and war.

"There is overwhelming evidence that the higher the level of self-esteem, the more likely it is to treat others with respect, kindness, and generosity."

My purpose through this text is to help you realize where you are now concerning your self-esteem and how you can create a healthier one.

We all have an idea about what self-esteem is. Sometimes, we do not believe we can live our life having healthy self-esteem. Most of us think people with high self-esteem are arrogant, and many of us have concluded that it is a taboo subject. But we should try to be happy and bring joy to the surrounding people.

How is our self-esteem created?

Our self-esteem is created by our family, teachers, friends, and society; it is determined by how we act with others, our relationships, work, and life. Self-esteem is based on how you view your abilities and dignity as a person.

Self-esteem focuses on how you feel about yourself.

People with low self-esteem feel bad about themselves, so they often live anxious and depressed lives. On the other hand, people with high self-esteem feel excellent. They are generally self-confident, knowing the importance of their care. It would be exciting to remember some things that we should not do when we begin to walk this path. Below, I will explain four crucial points in this regard:

1. Low self-esteem feeds on negative messages and thoughts; therefore, I suggest you not criticize yourself.

    When a critical thought pops into your mind, shift your attention, and think about something else; stop hurting yourself with your inner critic. Little by little, that inner critic will have less strength.

2. Low self-esteem feeds on the fear of being rejected, so don't try to please everyone all the time to feel accepted and loved. Remember that how you think is just as important as how others think, don't deny yourself.

3. Low self-esteem feeds on insecurity, so don't try to be like someone else.

   Remember, you are unique; you have special talents and ways of doing things; you can't be someone else if you are amazing.

   Always try to be a better person and compare yourself with your previous version, not with others.

4. Low self-esteem feeds on fear, so don't take things so seriously.

Remember, we never fail; there is no such thing as failure. People call failure simply the way they have found not to repeat things. Take the so-called failures as a learning process that leads you to where you want to get out of your comfort zone.

Exercises:

- Write down how you criticized yourself today.

- Write who you tried to please, who you wanted to make yourself look good today, and why you did it.

- Write down who you compared yourself to today and in what ways you did so.

- Write down something you consider you have failed at, why you think it is a failure, and how you feel.

- Write what you have learned from this failure.

- I recommend you repeat this exercise for twenty-one days in a row to make it a habit.

Happy new self-esteem.

THE ART OF MOTIVATING OTHERS

Knowing we deserve happiness is the most significant knowledge a human being can have in life. Therefore, I invite you to read this story whose message of hope can help you regain confidence; it is the metaphor of the crumpled bill.

This metaphor is a simple story that can be of great help.

The common denominator of all the versions of this peculiar motivational story is that no matter how crumpled a bill is, it still keeps its value.

THE CRUMPLED BILL

So many problems dejected Pablo's face because of the changes and family difficulties he was going through.

After so much thinking, he met his friend Laura at a restaurant for coffee.

Very depressed, he unloaded his anguish on her.

The job, the money, the crisis, his vocation, his failure, his frustrations. In short, everything seemed to be against him and very wrong in his life.

Laura listened patiently.

When Paul finished complaining and was waiting for comfort, she reached into her purse, pulled out a hundred-dollar bill, and said.

"Do you want this bill?"

Pablo, a little confused at first, answered her,

"Of course, Laura! It was a hundred dollars. Who doesn't want it?"

Then, Laura took the bill in one of her fists and crumpled it into a bit of a ball. Showing the crumpled ball to Pablo, she asked him again,

"And now, do you still want it?"

"Laura, I don't know what you want with this, but it's still a hundred dollars. Of course, I'll take it if you give it to me."

Laura unfolded the bill, threw it on the floor, and rubbed it against the floor with her shoe, lifting it dirty and marked.

Pablo remained still watching the scene, and, intrigued, he asked,

"Laura, I still don't understand where you're going with this, but this is a hundred-dollar bill, and as long as you don't tear it up, it retains its value."

Laura, staring at him, put her hand on his shoulder and said,

"Look, Pablo, this is the best example and gift I can give you. You must know that something does not go the way you want; even if life oppresses you, tramples you, frustrates you, or fails, you are still as valuable as you have always been. You should ask yourself how much you are worth; that will be your value and not how beaten you may be at any given moment. The most important thing is that no matter how you are, no matter what problems you have, you have a value, and you can keep it."

Paul stared at Laura without saying a word as the impact of the message penetrated deep into his heart.

He picked up the bill, excited, and gave it back to Laura; she, on the other hand, said to him:

"Keep it; this will be a great example for you to give to someone who has the same problem."

FOUR

CORDIALITY

Do you know what cordiality is?

C ordiality is a value that allows us to establish and maintain good relationships with others.

Cordiality is a synonym for kindness. A cordial person understands different cultures and is respectful to any person, no matter their beliefs.

When we are cordial, we solidify our relationships with the world and receive the good we long for by attraction.

Over time, the custom of teaching cordiality and kindness in the family has been lost.

When I was a child, my parents taught my siblings and me to ask for things please and thank you for the favors received — smiling when saying hello. To request permission to enter a place or take an object that is not ours, respect others, especially the elderly, and be gentlemanly with ladies and the elderly. For example, to give a seat to a senior citizen on a bus, open the door and give way to someone else, or put the garbage in its place.

I belong to that generation who grew up treating everyone well. It hurts me that, today, the same adults, that generation I grew up with, have forgotten all this. Today's children do not know how important it is to be polite to feel good about themselves.

Today, the same parents tell their children to throw the garbage out of the car window or on the floor.

When there was no trash can somewhere, my mother told us to put it in our pockets and, when we got home, to throw it in the trash can. Even as an adult, these are things that I have never forgotten.

It is up to us to make this a better world where civilized people live. No one is more or less than others; we are all human beings, no matter our social status, knowledge, or experience.

Stop complaining about governments, dirty cities, public transportation, jobs, salaries, and everything we say is wrong. Let's ask ourselves, what are we doing to change it? Nothing!

Let's start by changing our attitude, values, way of life, thoughts, and everything that makes a different environment. Let's practice daily cordiality and smile at the world every day. Let's be more empathetic and worry about caring more about people to create a change in ourselves. We will contribute to improving the world.

I feel good saying good morning, thank you, and asking for things please, and even if the other person does not answer me the same way, I smile. We will never know about the adversities that this other person is going through, and a simple smile or a kind word will make their burden less heavy, at least bearable.

THE GREETING

The greeting is the first sign of courtesy we offer when we are introduced to someone, enter a place, or meet a family member, a friend, or a superficial acquaintance.

There are some elementary rules:

When greeting, you should look into the person's eyes, constantly raising your forehead.

When entering a room, the person who arrives is naturally the one who should greet, and the one who leaves should say goodbye.

You should shake hands firmly but without being rude.

A too soft greeting, even given by a woman, does not leave a good impression.

It is not in good taste to kiss someone you do not know; it is enough to offer a handshake or introduce yourself by clearly pronouncing your name.

Under any circumstances, you should say hello.

Greet all the people you meet in a place, the doorman, the elevator operator, the receptionist, etc.

In a store, greet before requesting a service, or in a cab, before giving the address where you want to go.

Remember, the greeting is an easy way to express kindness and appreciation. Let's not forget it.

THE BEAUTY OF THE GREETING

There is a story about a man who worked in a meatpacking plant.

One day, at the end of his work schedule, he went to one of the coolers to inspect something. Suddenly, the door was locked, and he was trapped inside the cooler.

He banged loudly on the door and started yelling, but no one heard him.

Most of the workers had gone home, and it was almost impossible to hear him because of the thickness of the door.

He had been in the refrigerator for five hours and was on the verge of death.

Suddenly, the door opened. The security guard came in and rescued him.

Then he asked the guard,

"Why did it occur to you to open that door since it is not part of your work routine?"

He explained:

"I have been working in this company for thirty-five years. Hundreds of workers enter the plant every day, but you are the only one who greets me and says goodbye to me in the afternoon. The rest of the workers treat me as if I were invisible. Like every day, you said: 'Hello!' to me at the entrance, but I never heard: 'See you tomorrow!' and I look forward to that greeting and goodbye every day. Knowing that you had not yet said goodbye to me, I thought you must be somewhere in the building, so I looked for you and found you."

FIVE

GRATITUDE

A study published by the National Center for Biotechnology Information in the United States revealed that the brain is distracted by what it does not have. It can become uncomfortable for the person, instead of focusing on what it has and enjoying it.

It is called NEGATIVITY EFFECT; an example of this can be found in a beautiful field full of flowers, but in which someone has left some "forgotten" beer cans.

THE NEGATIVITY EFFECT will make the brain think the field is dirty and leave an acute perception, forgetting that 99% of that blanket of flowers is lush.

It explains why if we constantly focus on what we lack, we will go through stress, neediness, and a state of continued survival.

But it is not about "surviving" in the current society; it is about living and doing it in the best possible way.

THE NEGATIVITY EFFECT, which is studied in psychology, also makes people unhappier and mentally weaker, and more predisposed to diseases of all kinds.

Gratitude comprises actively thinking about what we have and for which we should be grateful.

Findings from the renowned Harvard University explain that gratitude is about people appreciating what they have. Rather than looking for something new, hoping it will make them happier or thinking. They cannot be satisfied until they get all their physical and material needs met.

Gratitude helps people focus on what they have instead of what they lack.

So, instead of focusing on everything wrong in your life, put gratitude into practice.

All you have to do is start thinking and actively looking, making efforts to become aware of the positives you should be grateful for. Do not let your brain have free rein to focus only on the negatives.

For example: thank you because I have a house, thank you because I have earned enough money to buy it, thank you because I am healthy enough to work, etc.

As with everything new incorporated into our daily habits, at first, it is logical to take a little effort to put this into practice. So, it will have to be done consciously, for example, by writing it down.

However, as it is practiced and executed consciously, logic dictates that this gratitude will show itself naturally. There will come a time when it will be done automatically.

To put this into practice, I suggest that every morning you dedicate at least six minutes to writing down the things for which you should feel grateful.

Thanks, because I have firm hands that allow me to grasp things and, simultaneously, sensitive hands to caress and sense my family and play instruments. Thanks, because I have legs and I can walk. Thanks, because I have two eyes. Thanks, because I have a family that loves me. Thanks, because I have siblings who help me when I need them. Thanks, because I meditated and found calm this morning. Thanks, because I have good food in the refrigerator, and so on.

With the practice of gratitude, you encourage the brain to find the positive and beneficial aspects of your life, bringing you a feeling of fulfillment, gratitude, optimism, and happiness.

Gratitude can be shown generically and in specific aspects of life.

The more specific it is, the more it is deepened, perceived, and felt.

The gratitude theory states that relationships become more satisfying by being grateful.

"THANK GOD FOR EVERYTHING"

MARIANO OSORIO

Once, a very wealthy person looked out his window and saw a man taking something out of the garbage, so he thought: "Thank God I am not poor."

The poor man looked up and saw a madman in rags wandering down the street and thought: "Thank God I'm not mad."

The madman looked ahead and saw an ambulance pass by and said to himself: "Thank God I am not sick."

Meanwhile, the sick man in the hospital saw a stretcher pass by with a body under a sheet and said to himself: "Thank God I am alive."

Only the dead man could thank nothing.

Why don't you thank God today for all the blessings you have received, the gift of life, and this beautiful day?

WHAT IS LIFE?

To better understand what life is, you have to visit three places: a hospital, a prison, and a cemetery.

In the hospital, you will see nothing more beautiful than health.

In prison, you will see there is nothing more precious than freedom.

In the cemetery, you will understand that, in life, what counts are your good spiritual deeds, nothing else.

The ground you walk on today will be your roof tomorrow.

The sad truth is that we all arrive with nothing and will leave with nothing.

We should be humble in front of God and thank Him every day for all we are and all we have.

What about you? Why do you feel so grateful to God today?

"then the Lord knoweth how to deliver the godly out of temptations and to reserve the unjust unto the Day of Judgment to be punished."

2 Peter 2:9
KJ21

"casting all your cares upon Him, for He careth for you."

1 Peter 5: 7
KJ21

"Jesus Christ is the same yesterday, and today, and forever."

Hebrews 13:8
KJ21

"The discretion of a man deferreth his anger, and it is his glory to pass over a transgression."

Proverbs 19:11
KJ21

"The Lord upholdeth all that fall, and raiseth up all those that are bowed down."

Psalm 145:14
KJ21

SIX

COMPASSION

Compassion is a human feeling that manifests itself through contact with others and the comprehension of their suffering.

It is more intense than empathy; it is the perception of the suffering of our fellow human beings and the desire to alleviate, reduce or eliminate their painful situation.

Compassionate action makes us feel good. For example, when you see a homeless person and give them food and clothing, it is like a vaccine against their distress, increasing their hope and resilience.

One morning, as I walked through New Orleans downtown on my way to work, I spotted a handicapped man a few feet away, sweating and struggling to move his wheelchair. I approached him and noticed he was exhausted, so I offered to help him push his chair.

I pushed him approximately eight blocks to the transportation terminal, where he boarded a bus that would take him home.

Being in solidarity and helping that person made me experience a great sense of happiness and love for others.

Next, I will share a story where the protagonist invites us to be more compassionate with others.

THE POWER OF NEIGHBORLY LOVE

A wealthy Japanese widower decided to retire from the city and go to the highest part, overlooking the sea.

He built a beautiful mansion with splendid views of the horizon and was very happy, surrounded by beauty and solitude.

He liked to gaze at the beach and watch people enjoying the sun and the water.

In his solitude, he discovered a deeper meaning of love.

He would come down from the mountain and mingle with the city's people from time to time.

He felt a particular concern for the elderly and the poor. On different occasions, he would quietly help families in financial difficulty. He came to love that community.

Besides watching the people enjoying the beach, he spent many hours observing, through a powerful telescope, the movement of the sea animals and the ships that sailed there.

One day, he saw gigantic waves possibly resulting from a tsunami, so he frantically shouted at the people on the beach.

Unfortunately, they could not hear him, so, in desperation. He set fire to his beautiful mansion, hoping that by seeing the flames burn, people would climb up the steep hills to help him so that they could escape the giant waves.

The people on the beach saw the flames spread across the roof of that mansion.

Someone shouted to everyone on the beach:

"Let's climb the steep hills and help our friend put out the fire!" Many responded to this call for help, but others just said, "We are having a great time here... You go and help him."

Soon, the gigantic waves came ashore and swept the entire beach out to sea—those who were there drowned. Others, moved by an act of love for the widower, reached higher ground and were saved from the fury of the waves.

The power of love is valuable; nothing in this world can do more than love.

SEVEN

EMPATHY

E mpathy is the ability to put ourselves in another person's shoes, listen to them, and understand them sincerely. It is a virtue that increases with practice and is fundamental to good communication.

Living with empathy is simple; it is a matter of stopping to think a little about others. As a result, we will learn to act favorably in all circumstances.

Therefore, we must be attentive and take care of the small details that reaffirm this value in our person.

Always try to smile; this generates an atmosphere of trust and cordiality that leaves the person without the possibility of a negative response, surprising them.

Consider as important first the issues of others and then your own.

After listening to the person who has approached you, that person will surely be able to understand your situation and your state of mind. So, they will be willing to help you.

Please do not make a premature judgment of people, making you change your inner disposition towards them. Don't think things like: "this sourpuss is here," "he's at it again," "he won't leave me alone," and "another setback." If someone comes to you, they need someone to talk to... don't discourage them.

If you do not have time or it is a wrong moment, express it with courtesy and delicacy; that is also empathy. People will feel equally cared for and necessary, but do not let too much time pass to chat with the person.

Avoid showing haste, boredom, tiredness, giving blunt answers, or being distracted by other things. These are disrespectful; show self-control and interest in people and learn to listen.

Do not forget to instill encouragement with words, a pat on the shoulder, or a kind gesture, especially if the person is in trouble; it always lifts the mood.

In conclusion, empathy is a significant value to strengthen in all aspects of our life; without it, it would be tough to enrich our interpersonal relationships.

In this sense, those who care about living with this value simultaneously cultivate trust, friendship, comprehension, generosity, respect, and communication.

We must not forget that modernity and its life pace provide few opportunities to serve and understand others, get to know them, and treat them properly.

Empathy is necessary to get closer and make our relationships more human. It is a fundamental piece that enriches us and identifies us as better human beings.

As a complement to this chapter, I will share a beautiful story about the value of empathy.

THE HOSPITAL WINDOW

This anonymous story entitled The Hospital Window tells us how you can get so much from other people with very little. How, with imagination, you can ignite the spark of illusion and life?

It speaks of kindness, compassion, and positive thinking.

It speaks of solidarity and, above all, empathy.

It is a beautiful story full of values that people of all ages should have that will fill you up inside.

Two older men shared a room in a hospital. Both were very ill, but one of them could still get up from time to time to look out of the window next to his bed. However, the other older man was bedridden and barely had the strength to sit up.

The two of them kept talking, telling each other a thousand stories of their past and present. They held each other company and spoke about their lives, what they did and didn't do, their dreams fulfilled, and those they never got to see.

But the favorite moment for both of them all day was when the man at the window would look out the glass and narrate to his roommate everything. He saw through it:

"It's a beautiful day! The park is filling up with children laughing so. Happily, couples arriving with their hands clasped... The willows are lush, and butterflies are fluttering among the flowers. Oh, my friend, what a beautiful garden we have out there! It has a pond with crystal clear water and birds that come shyly to drink..."

And while the man narrated what he saw, his companion closed his eyes and tried to imagine everything he heard. He smiled and noticed great inner peace and happiness.

Every day, his companion narrated what he saw, and he got an idea of the picture. He told him an orchestra was outside one summer evening, and wagons were parading by. What fun they were having! And so, **the days seemed less gray**, less harsh, and kinder.

Until one day or one morning, the nurse found the **man's lifeless body** next to the window.

Everyone was very sorry for his loss, but especially his roommate.

After a few days, he asked to be moved to the bed by the window. He wanted to see everything that his roommate so enthusiastically told him about. The doctors granted his wish; despite the pain, he sat up to look out the window once in bed.

But..., what did her eyes see, and the park, where was the pond, and the willows? To his surprise, the window only looked out onto a **white wall**...

Then he asked the nurse, "Why was my partner narrating all those stories about a park if it doesn't exist?" The nurse looked at him sympathetically.

Replying, he was blind; he couldn't even see the wall.

She said: "Maybe he just wanted to cheer you up."

REFLECTIONS ON THIS BEAUTIFUL STORY

We have an enormous capacity to transform the people we are close to, make them happy, and get them to experience life.

That does not cost much, but rather, little.

That is what the protagonist of this story did with his imaginary narratives:

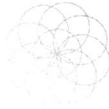

TO MAKE THE OTHER HAPPY

Every day, the patient at the window imagined for his companion an ideal world in which happiness was genuinely contagious.

It is not that he lied, but that he created a distinct reality that fed **his illusion**, desire to live, and love life.

And the illusion of what we do not see but can imagine and sometimes feel is the fuel we need to keep fighting. **Faith and fantasy in what we cannot see**: children live from their imagination and **are happy**.

Sometimes, it is better to ignore what distresses us or causes us sadness. It is necessary to transform it into something that fills us with hope; this is essential to move forward.

We all need something that encourages us to help us continue loving life.

We all look for something that fills us with energy and vitality that helps us to strengthen our positive thinking.

Because happiness can only be achieved with positivity.

Our protagonist knew they were both in the wrong way, but he thought his companion also had something against him: he couldn't get up.

He could be their contact with reality. But... why not transform it a little? Why not give it something extraordinary so that he could smile every day?

Imagine if the man in the window had been realistic and sincere; what would he have told his partner that he only saw a sad white wall every day?

Both would have been depressed, don't you think? Far from that, he chose to imagine an ideal world that would allow them both to be happy when they had left. A world that he also wanted to share with his partner to infect him with his happiness.

EIGHT

SUFFERING AFTER REJECTION

A FATHER'S ADVICE

Who is exempt from suffering?

O ur life is framed by suffering; no one is exempt from it; in this life, we all suffer in different ways, some more and others less; only God knows how it touches each one of us.

Suffering is a material, physical, moral, or spiritual affliction that makes someone sad, anxious, and lonely. People who experience physical suffering may feel unable to cope with daily life, perhaps because of an illness.

Suffering teaches us we cannot control our circumstances, but we can maintain our attitude toward them... To stop suffering, we need to know ourselves and learn to be the protagonists of our lives instead of being victims of our thoughts. Now I will share one of the stages of my life in which I was a victim of suffering.

Some time ago, I was building my house in the city of La Ceiba, on the north coast of Honduras. The house was constructed according to a colonial-style sketch I designed. When the work was finished, the neighbors and most people who observed it admired it.

The house floor had a height of approximately one meter, a detail that made it look like a unique design. In the early morning hours, a group of builders prepared the roof structure hard at work.

At that time, I lived with my sister Marieta; her house was right next to mine, which was still under construction. One day, my father came to visit us. Marieta prepared us a succulent breakfast. My father asked me how the structure of my house was going while eating our food, exchanging anecdotes related to daily life issues in the conversation.

That was the moment I took the opportunity to invite him to look at the construction site. So, we walked a little over thirty meters until we were in front of the building. We both gazed in ecstasy at the residence. Suddenly, my father interrupted the silence and asked me, "Son, what material will you use to complete the roof of your house?"

"With asbestos, Dad," I answered.

"Are you going to put asbestos on your house?" my father asked again.

"Yes, Dad," I answered, "why asbestos is a very cool material. Besides, it will give a better appearance at the house," I added.

"Son," said my father, "a friend of mine has a newly built house in Trujillo-city and the municipality of Honduras. Just a month ago, he changed the asbestos roof of his house for an aluzinc one. The first one deteriorated and when it rained, the water leaked everywhere. I suggest you put aluzinc on your house," said my father.

"No, Dad," I replied, "I have always dreamed of having a house with an asbestos roof, and I am unwilling to give up that dream."

My father, noticing my attitude, sadly told me, "I am only trying to prevent you from having a bad time with your house," my father affirmed.

I immediately changed the subject, ignoring my father's loving warning. Two years after our marriage, I lived in the house with my wife, where our children were born, and we also had a niece, making up a family of seven members.

The strong winter hit the nine-year-old house; it was raining cats and dogs, and a water leak appeared in the ceiling above the hallway. The bedrooms leaked. Suddenly, another one appeared in the dining room. The next day, we discovered another in the children's rooms, so we put containers to recycle the seeping water from the cracks.

When there was an opportunity, I would climb up on the roof to patch the holes I found, but there were many more leaks the next day than I needed to fix. One morning, I climbed up on the roof to patch as many cracks as possible. I discovered a hole of 1 inch in diameter, but there was a very particular leak this time. I stood in an area with no support, so it was not the water that leaked but myself; I opened a hole of 3 feet in diameter. By the work of God, I fell on the inner wall of the room. As a result of the accident, I had to replace the entire sheeting to repair the damage.

I would like this to be the end of this story, but it is only the beginning. One day, we reached a point where the water leaked down the wall. It made it impossible for us to recycle it. It flooded the children's room and went up 2 inches. One night, while it was raining heavily, I left my bed and went to my children's room to help them go to the bathroom. As I looked out the room door, I saw several of my children's items floating, sandals, shoes, and toys swimming in the water. I felt unfortunate to see my children put their little feet in the cold pool of water that formed in their room.

At that moment, memories of my father, who had advised me not to put asbestos on the roof of my house, came to my mind, and I dismissed them. No matter how hard I tried, I could not prevent tears from flowing from my eyes as I lived and witnessed that tragic scene. And so, the days, weeks, and months went by. In addition to the roof's difficulties and deterioration, the workflow in the welding area, our primary source of income, had decreased drastically. My savings were depleted in the immediate household expenses.

The little income was spent immediately on food supplies and fixed household expenses. At a certain point, I felt helpless. But I never lost faith, hope, and love in the Divine Creator of the universe. Through this experience, I learned not to reject the good advice my father used to give me.

HOW DID I OVERCOME THE CRISIS?

My first step was to prostrate myself before God in deep prayer to overcome the crisis. At that moment, I came up with making a plan; I would ask for a loan to get the money I needed to repair the house. Then I looked for a mason and asked him to give me an estimate to change the house's roof; I asked him to include the total cost, material, and labor.

Once I knew how much it would cost to complete the project, I applied for a loan from a cooperative.

When the loan was approved, I had the deteriorated asbestos roof removed and replaced it with an aluzinc roof, as my father had advised me.

Today I enjoy the sound of the rain falling on the house's roof.

Next, I will share a beautiful reflection that will guide you and help you grow in this journey through life.

IMPOSSIBLE TO GO THROUGH LIFE

AUTHOR ANONYMOUS

One grows

Impossible to go through life...

without a job going wrong,

without a friendship causing disappointment,

without suffering some health breakdown,

without a love leaving us,

without anyone in the family passing away,

without making a mistake in a business deal.

That... That is the cost of living.

However, it is not what happens which is essential,

but how you react.

If you collect eternally bleeding wounds, you will live like a
wounded bird, unable to fly again,

you will live like a wounded bird, unable to fly again.

One grows...

One grows when there is no emptiness of hope,

nor weakening of will, nor loss of faith.

One grows when one accepts the reality

and has the poise to live it.

When you accept your destiny,

but have the will to change it.

You grow by assimilating what you leave behind,

building what lies ahead,

and projecting what may be the future.

One grows when one overcomes, values oneself, and

knows how to bear fruit.

One grows when one opens paths, leaves footprints,

internalizes experiences... and plant's roots!

You grow when you set goals for yourself,

regardless of negative comments and prejudices.

When you set examples regardless of ridicule and scorn

when you do your job.

One grows when one is strong by character,

sustained by training, sensitive by temperament

and human by birth!

You grow when you face the winter,

even if it loses its leaves,

gathers flowers, even if they have thorns, and

marks paths, even if the dust rises.

One grows when one can reach oneself

with residues of illusions,

capable of perfuming oneself with residues of flowers...

and to ignite oneself with residues of love!...

One grows by helping one's fellow men,

knowing oneself and giving

to life more than it receives.

One grows when one plants oneself so as not to retreat.

When one defends oneself like an eagle, not stop flying.

When it anchors like an anchor and shines like a star.

Then... then it is **when one grows**.

One grows when one surrenders

from the heart to God's purposes...

One grows by letting the Lord

accompany you throughout your life.

NINE

GENTLENESS

Gentleness and kindness are paramount in human relations these days. Sometimes, we are treated with indifference when we visit certain commercial establishments or state institutions. It awakened my interest in the subject of kindness; I researched and found an article about the International Day of Service that I now share with you.

World Kindness Day was born in 1977 in Tokyo (Japan), where the idea of dedicating this day to sharing positivism and making others happy was promoted. This day is celebrated in several countries, including Japan, the United States, Canada, and Mexico. Every year, more countries join in celebrating it.

Acts of kindness or gentleness can be different for each person; the objective is to be able to help our fellow men and women without asking for anything in return.

On November 13, World Kindness Day is celebrated. The idea is to make a call to perform acts of kindness that contribute to the happiness and well-being of oneself and others. Among its benefits is facilitating interpersonal relationships. Being kind also helps to develop that capacity for self-control over moods. In addition, scientific studies done by researchers at the University of Michigan in 2003 indicate that practicing kindness prolongs life. It creates new neural connections and stimulates the production of endorphins, leading to an increased sense of well-being.

I will now share a list of actions you can take starting this day.

1. **Smile.** Smiling can fill spaces that words sometimes cannot load. It conveys a sense of companionship and pleasure in sharing or identifying with others. While a child may smile four hundred times a day, one in three adults smiles over twenty, and about 50% of people don't smile back at a stranger. You could also share your best joke - why not.

2. **Always use magic words.** Use them with conviction in front of acquaintances and strangers. Those that open minds and hearts: please, thank you, excuse me, with your permission, at your service, bon appétit!

3. **Practice courtesy.** Along with the magic words, say hello and goodbye by looking into the eyes, answer calls, don't keep people waiting, and be punctual.

4. **Yield your place.** Inline at the supermarket, at the cinema, in traffic, on public transport, in a coffee shop...

5. **Spend some of your money on others.** Whether or not you know it. It could be candy, a drink, a souvenir, a book, or paying a toll... Serious studies have shown that investing in others generates levels of well-being and satisfaction that are much more sustained over time than when spent on yourself.

6. **Give the gift of time.** Pay a visit or share something to express affection or listen, visit or call a sick or a lonely person.

7. **Practice "appreciability."** This term is understood as the ability to see everything and deliberately select the best and most appreciated. According to Laura Isanta, co-founder of the Argentina-based Instituto del Bienestar, you should ask yourself this fundamental question: how do you want to live your life? Looking for the best or the worst in people.

8. **Surprise.** Think of something that favors someone and do it tomorrow. Besides the satisfaction it generates in the other person, note what happens to your mood.

For example, I'll share how I did it.

One morning while I was praying, intense experiences came to my mind. Because of the scarcity of economic resources, I worked as a waiter with my friends in three of the best hotels in La Ceiba, my home country, Honduras. Many years had passed without having the opportunity to communicate with my colleagues.

So, I made a long-distance call to one of the hotels, and I asked the receptionist to put me through to one of my waiter colleagues who still worked in the company. On that occasion, it was the Christmas season. In our Hispanic American culture, Christmas is celebrated by preparing and enjoying an abundance and variety of food and beverages.

So, I asked my friend to send me a list of all the former fellow waiters who still work at the hotel company where this server worked for several years. I transferred him several dollars, equivalent to two days of my work, and asked him to distribute it in equal parts among all the names on the list.

It is not that I am a millionaire or that I have enough money to give it away. Still, when my friends thanked me for the gift, I had given them, it caused me great emotion and pleasure; I had practiced showing love for my fellow men.

A proverb says: "There is no one so poor that he has nothing to give, nor is there anyone so rich that he has nothing to receive."

TEN

THE GRACE AND PHILANTHROPY OF WILL SMITH

What is philanthropy?

The term **philanthropy** designates love for the human species and for everything that humanity is concerned with. It is expressed in the unselfish help to others or an attitude of support through donations, such as clothes, food, and money that collaborate in the solution of the problems of others.

I will share a story about the renowned actor, Will Smith.

Several media outlets stated that a city in Louisiana would not have fireworks display on July 4, 2021, as is customary to celebrate the Independence Day of the United States. There were economic problems that prevented it. The philanthropic actor Will Smith was in New Orleans at the time, working on the movie Emancipation, and found out about the situation. So, he took the sum of one hundred thousand dollars out of his pocket and donated it to the city so the celebration with fireworks could take place, as usual, on the Mississippi River.

Will had a sympathetic gesture with his temporary neighbors and did not allow them to overlook this celebration for the second consecutive year due to lack of funds, as in 2020 for the COVID-19 pandemic.

The locals posted their pictures on social networks and showed their gratitude to the philanthropic actor Will Smith. Below, I share with you this reflection.

ANYWAY

Sometimes people behave unreasonably, unconsciously, and selfishly; forgive them anyway...

If you are kind, they accuse you of having dark, selfish motives; be kind anyway...

If you are successful, you will gain false friends and true enemies; be successful anyway...

If you are sincere, people can cheat you; be sincere anyway...

What takes you years to build, someone could destroy it in one night; build anyway...

If you find tranquility and happiness, they might envy you; be happy anyway...

Many will have forgotten tomorrow the good you do today; do good anyway...

Give to the world the best you have, and it may never be enough; give to the world the best you have, anyway...

ELEVEN

WILL SMITH IN NEW ORLEANS

O ne cool morning, while I walked through the French neighborhood in New Orleans, the United States, towards the Monteleone Hotel. I enjoyed watching how the gentle breeze was swaying the bushes and the beautiful flowers in the flower boxes that adorn the hotel's windows, creating a climate of peace and harmony. Suddenly I stepped on an object that induced me to look at the ground. I discovered it was a bunch of cables; I looked up, trying to see where they came from. They were coming out of the several trucks park at the edge of Iberville Street.

On each truck was a substantial, white-lettered sign that read HOLLYWOOD.

The opposite end of the wires led to the Monteleone Hotel facility.

The Monteleone is a five-star hotel that is very important in the history of New Orleans, was nominated by the City Business magazine for the Best Places to Work award, for being a hotel that stands out for its antiquity and its historical value within the city.

Today, many of its employees have been with the company for many years, such as Mrs. Katy, who is 50; Mr. Al, 62; others are 25, 30, and 40. The Monteleone Hotel holds a special place in American culture.

Legendary literary greats such as Tennessee Williams, William Faulkner, and other famous Hollywood actors and actresses have dined and drank on the premises.

Books have been written there, and several films have been shot there.

I entered the hotel through the back and went to the employee's dressing room in the building's basement. I got dressed and suddenly heard noises coming from the upper floor, which increased my curiosity to know the reason for the commotion.

As soon as I got into my waiter's uniform, I looked in the mirror, ensuring I was adequately dressed. I was wearing black pants, a white long-sleeved shirt, a tie, black shoes, and a black vest.

At chest level, on the left side, I was wearing a golden name tag with my name on it, which read Arles.

Then I moved to the place where the time clock was located, marked the time of entry, and immediately moved to the restaurant where I worked as a back server.

Upon arriving at the Criollo Restaurant, distinguished by its excellent gastronomy, most of my colleagues were crowded near the bar. I approached the group and heard them laughing, smiling, and commenting about the famous actors and actresses circulating in the restaurant and bar area.

Also, from the entrance to the hotel, there were many Hollywood cameramen bustling about on the second floor of the building. A large amount of film equipment was scattered all over the place; they were scattered from Royal Street to the inside of the Carrousel bar.

The Carousel Piano Bar and Lounge is the only revolving bar in New Orleans, named one of the top twenty bars in the world for its atypical circus-like infrastructure.

The movement of people made me more curious, so much so that I subtly inquired why there was so much bustle in the hotel.

When I found out they were filming scenes from the movie Girls Trip.

The movie starred actresses Regina Hall, Tiffany Haddish, and Jada Pinkett, wife of actor Will Smith.

The bar and the restaurant are divided by a wall. It is formed by two screens painted in gray and installed in parallel with a separation of two meters between the two pieces, which, at the same time, serve as access to the two rooms.

Meanwhile, some onlookers were trying to spy on what was going on in the bar in the restaurant. Others were moving erratically, trying to see as many actors and actresses as possible in the hotel, which generated a comfortable atmosphere.

Suddenly, I saw a character that stood out for his athletic build; I realized it was the renowned actor, Will Smith.

Seeing my gesture of astonishment, he approached me and, with a broad smile, extended his hand, shaking mine, and greeted me.

I reciprocated and asked him to take a picture with me. The actor gladly agreed to my request, so I told one of my companions to take our picture. I tried to thank him, but in surprise! He anticipated and expressed these words with a subtle tone of voice: "Thank you, thank you, my brother, thank you for taking a picture with me."

My dear reader, Will Smith's act of gentleness and kindness made me reflect on his outstanding qualities as a human being. Preaching through example, he gave me an essential lesson about human values. His humility showed me his knowledge that all people are necessary.

Since then, I have focused on developing my human virtues and, at the same time, helping my fellow human beings as I am doing with you through this book that you hold in your hands.

TWELVE

TRUE WISDOM

Wisdom is developed by applying intelligence to one's own experience, drawing conclusions that give us greater understanding and enable us to reflect and gain the discernment that leads us to know the truth and recognize right from wrong.

I have written about this subject so that all people who love authentic wisdom can lead a life much more by the natural law of God.

It is not wiser the one who knows the most, but the one who loves the most because love is precisely the fruit of the one who possesses authentic wisdom. If there is love in you, then there is wisdom. In his letter in chapter three, the apostle James speaks of two types of wisdom, and each has its fruits. The wisdom that does not come from heaven but evil has three characteristics: earthly, sensual, and demonic. We must realize that the spirit of Satan can also bestow wisdom to confuse and lead the children of God through byways of seduction, sensual and earthly attractive of this world.

But the Bible says the wisdom that comes from God has other characteristics. It is peaceful wisdom, blameless, and full of patience, compassion, mercy, and fruitful love. That instills in your soul the holy fear of God: respect and love for our Heavenly Father above all things.

In discovering that there are two types of wisdom, the Lord invites us to define ourselves. There are two paths, and it will depend on you which one you want to take. There is implicit fornication, impurity, sensuality, and idolatry; it provokes hatred, discord, resentment, divisions, sectarianism, jealousy, envy, greed, and avarice. Moreover, it also stimulates selfishness, quarreling, drunkenness, carousing, and similar things, because it does not proceed from God. If there is any of this in you, realize that you are on the wrong path of wisdom.

The Lord in the book of Proverbs 1:7 tells us that true wisdom comes from God and only fools despise the discipline and understanding that comes from heaven and leads to glory.

Jesus is the one who should animate your thoughts. He is the father's wisdom incarnate, who encourages you to pronounce sweet words. Your behavior is kind, and your way of looking, listening, and conducting yourself in life is noble.

True wisdom comes from God and is found in a life of prayer. A soul that communes with God's love every morning is a wise person. On the next page, I will share a beautiful reflection on wisdom.

EVIL DOES NOT EXIST BY ITSELF

This story took place in Germany at the beginning of the 20th century. During a lecture with several university students, a professor at the University of Berlin proposed a challenge for the students with the following question:

"Did God create everything that exists?"

One student bravely answered:

"Yes, he created everything that exists, yes sir," replied the young man.

The teacher said:

"If God created everything that exists, then God did evil, since evil exists! And if we say that our works reflect ourselves, then God is evil because he created evil."

The young man was silent before that explanation by the professor, who rejoiced to have proved, once again, that faith was a myth.

Another student raised his hand and said,

"Can I ask you a question, professor?"

"Of course, you may," was the professor's reply.

The young man stood up and asked,

"Professor, does cold exist?"

"But what kind of question is that? Of course, it exists, or have you never felt cold?" said the professor.

The boy replied,

"Sir, there is no such thing as cold. According to the laws of physics, what we consider "cold" is the absence of heat. Everybody or an object is feasible to study when it possesses or transmits energy; heat makes a body possess or transmit energy. Absolute zero is the total absence of heat; all bodies remain inert, unable to react, but cold does not exist. We created that definition to describe how we feel when we have no heat."

"And is there such a thing as darkness?" continued the student.

The professor answered,

"It exists."

The student replied,

"Darkness does not exist, either. Darkness is the absence of light. The light we can study, darkness, no! Through Nicol's prism, white light can be broken into various colors with different wavelengths. Darkness, no! How can you tell how dark a given space is? Based on the amount of light present in that space, right? Darkness is a definition used by man to describe what happens when light is absent."

Finally, the young man asked the professor,

"Sir, does evil exist?"

The professor answered,

"Of course, it exists; as I mentioned initially, we see rapes, crimes, and violence worldwide; those are evil things."

The student replied,

"Evil does not exist, sir, or at least it does not exist unto itself. Evil is simply the absence of God... According to the previous cases, evil is a definition that man invented to describe the absence of God. He did not create evil; it results from the absence of God in the hearts of human beings. It is the same as what happens with cold when there is no heat, or darkness when there is no light."

The young man received a standing ovation, and the professor, shaking his head, remained silent...

The director of the university turned to the young student and asked,

"What is your name?"

The boy answered,

"My name is ALBERT EINSTEIN."

THIRTEEN

FAMILY INDIFFERENCE

Family indifference occurs when one spouse does not make a bond effectively with the rest of the family.

This attitude may include physical, psychological, or other types of abuse.

Family indifference exists in a household if there is a repetitive attitude of indifference, not because of a single isolated event.

The victim of family indifference can be any person who is considered a member of the offender's family or who has lived with the offender somehow.

Indifference is mainly associated with the aggressor's insensitivity, detachment, or coldness. Generally, the aggressor has no capacity for self-control and acts as if his emotions and feelings were anesthetized.

As an illustration of this, I will share a story that, if you reflect on it, will help you improve your family relationship.

I'M SICK OF LIFE

MARIANO OSORIO

I am tired of working and seeing the same people; I walk to work every day; I get home, and my wife serves the same thing for dinner, which I don't like very much, but I have to eat the food I don't like.

I go into the bathroom, and my daughter, who is only a year and a half old, won't let me because she wants to play with me; she doesn't understand I'm tired, and I want to go into the bathroom. Afterward, I take my magazine to read it in my armchair, and my daughter wants to play again and be lulled in my arms; I want to read my magazine, and my wife comes out with her...

"How do I look? I dressed up for you." I tell her, okay, but I don't take my eyes off my magazine for good measure. She gets mad at me and says that I don't understand her and never listen to her. I wonder why she gets mad if I give her all my attention, even when watching TV. Of course, I pay attention to her, as long as there are bad commercials.

Sometimes, I wish I could be alone and not listen to anything; I want to rest; I have enough problems at work to listen to those at home. My father also bothers me sometimes, and between clients, wife, daughter, and father, they drive me crazy; I want peace!

The only good thing is to sleep. When I close my eyes, I feel a great relief as I forget everything and everyone, until...

"Hello, I've come for you. "

"Who are you? How did you get in?"

"God sent me for you; he said he heard your complaints, and you're right; it's time to rest."

"That's not possible, for that I would have to be..."

"That's right. Yes, you are. You won't worry anymore about seeing the same people walking, putting up with your wife with her stews, or your little daughter bothering you. Even more, you'll never listen to your father's advice."

"But what will happen with everything, with my work?"

"Don't worry, in your company; they already hired another person to fill your position, and, by the way, he is pleased because he didn't have a job."

"What about my wife and my baby?"

"Your wife was given a good man who loves, respects, and admires her for the qualities you never observed in her. He gladly accepts all her food without complaining about anything because of thanks to God and her. He has something to put in his mouth every day, unlike other people who have nothing to eat and go hungry, even for months. Besides, he cares about your daughter and loves her as if she were his own, and, no matter how tired he always comes home from work, he takes time to play with her; they are pleased."

"No, it can't be... -No! No! No! I can't be dead!"

"I'm sorry, the decision has been made."

"But... that means I will never again kiss my baby's face, never again say "I love you" to my wife, never again see my friends tell them how much I appreciate them or hug my father. I will no longer live; I will no longer exist. I will be buried in the cemetery, and my body will remain there, covered with earth. I will never again hear the words they used to say to me: 'Hey, my friend, you are the best,' 'my son, I am proud of you,' 'how much I love my husband,' or 'daddy, I love you very much..."

"No, no, no, no, I don't want to die, I want to live, I want to grow old with my wife, I don't want to die yet!"

"But that's what you wanted, to rest! Now you've got your eternal rest, sleep... forever..."

"No, no, no, no, no, no, I don't want to! God, please, God! No, please!"

"Hey, hey, what's the matter, love? You're having a nightmare," said my wife, waking me up from this horrible dream.

"No, it wasn't a nightmare, my love; it was another chance to enjoy you, my baby, my family, everything God has created. You know, being dead, you can't do anything, and being alive, you can enjoy everything."

FOURTEEN

FORGIVENESS

Forgiveness is a decision and also a process; it is not something instantaneous. To forgive, we must struggle to overcome our arrogance, pride, and fear of ignoring people, not their actions.

We must be aware the act of forgiving does not mean denying reality. We must not allow ourselves to be mistreated or hurt physically or mentally; we must set limits. We can forgive and distance ourselves from those who lead us astray and pray for them.

Forgiving our friends has great merit, but forgiving our enemies has an even greater value and a much more significant benefit for ourselves, for our health, and, above all, for our spiritual good. Here is a reflection of forgiveness.

HEALING THROUGH FORGIVENESS

A lady was looking with great interest for the parish priest to unburden herself and ask him for advice; she was feeling sick, both in body and soul. She had an ulcer in her stomach and was afraid to have an operation.

When she met the priest, she asked him,

"Father, do you think if I offer a prayer or some penance, my ulcer can be healed without having an operation?"

The priest answered with another question:

"Madam, is there anyone you hate?"

The lady answered, "Yes, father, but it is a justified hatred, and I do not intend to forgive that person. I have every reason to hate her; she offended me very much."

The priest then said to her, "Once Jesus taught that there is no merit in doing good to those who do good to us because anyone does that. True nobility of the soul consists in repaying with good those who do us wrong. It applies in this case. It is not a question of whether hatred is justified; if you have reasons, then the greater the merits of forgiving. Otherwise, by making prayers or offering sacrifices, I doubt it will alleviate your ulcer."

The woman remained thoughtful, then they prayed together, and the woman left.

When she got home, she told her husband what had happened; he also asked her to forgive the person who had offended her. She resisted, but he insisted: "Let's pray so that you can forgive." In the middle of the prayer, she surrendered, and immediately, a calm and great peace came over her. The woman continued to pray daily.

A few weeks later, the woman went to the hospital for further tests and to set a date for the operation if it was still necessary. The doctor told her the ulcer had inexplicably disappeared. This woman's condition had been caused by the hatred of another person. The hatred having disappeared, the disease also disappeared.

POPE JOHN PAUL II
FORGIVES HIS AGGRESSOR

At 5:17 p.m. on May 13, 1981, John Paul II had just returned a little girl to her parents after having hugged and blessed her during the audience in front of some thirty thousand faithful in St. Peter's Square in the heart of Vatican City. Mehmet Ali Ağca, a twenty-three-year-old Turkish young man who shot at the Pope's body three meters away with a nine-millimeter caliber semi-automatic gun, left him seriously wounded.

In 1983, the pope visited the prison where the man who may have been his murderer served a life sentence. The pontiff looked Mehmet in his eyes, and Mehmet took his hand and kissed it. John Paul II sat and talked with him for a long time.

The pope gave him a rosary. After their talk, he assured him, "the things they talked about would be kept secret between the two of them. They talked like two brothers, and he forgave him, giving him his full confidence."

Years later, the pope was gravely ill, and when the news reached Turkey, Mehmet's lawyer stated that his client "is unfortunate. He thinks of his brother, the pope, and prays for him."

On April 2, 2005, John Paul II died. Five years later, Mehmet was pardoned, and in 2014, he went to St. Peter's Square for the second time in his life. But this time, he carries no weapons. This time he had two dozen white roses and laid them on the tomb of John Paul II.

The police stopped him for questioning, and Mehmet said: "I felt the need to make this gesture."

Thus, God attacks the most beautiful story of forgiveness in the world.

FIFTEEN

INDULGENCE

O nce upon a time, I read a book by Robert Kiyosaki. The author tells us about his experience of loving and forgiving the enemy.

Robert Kiyosaki is an American entrepreneur, investor, writer, lecturer, and motivational speaker of Japanese descent.

He is the founder, director, CEO, and majority shareholder of Cashflow Technologies Corporation, which holds the license to the Rich Dad, Poor Dad brand. Robert shares with us a fraction of his spiritual life and gives us some examples that help us develop our character. He also shows us the importance of forgiving and loving others.

THERE ARE NO ATHEISTS IN THE TRENCHES

In Vietnam, the night before each mission, I would go alone to the bow of the aircraft carrier and sit there in silence.

I would be quiet for an hour and listen to the colossal bow slicing through the waves.

It was very relaxing to remain in silence. At the same time, the ship ascended and descended in harmony with the swell of the sea.

There I would meditate, become the spirit of God, and pray for a few minutes for my crew.

We did it with courage and love when we flew and became one. Likewise, before each mission, I remembered my mother's wish for me to visit the church, and I realized how important it was to her.

One day, we did an emergency medical evacuation.

A young sailor stepped on a personal mine, and we flew him by helicopter to the hospital.

He had lost his leg, was hemorrhaging heavily, and kept calling out for his mother as life left him.

Shortly before we arrived at the hospital, he stopped calling for her. We all cried as the doctors removed his lifeless body from the helicopter.

I went for a walk and found a private place where I could thank my mom, who had passed away two years earlier when I was still in-flight school in Florida.

Every night before a mission, I would sit on the bow of the aircraft carrier and include her in my thoughts and prayers.

The following day, I would fly with her in my heart. A month later, while on base in a remote field, I discovered several boys planting sacks with explosive charges on our ship. Immediately, I connected them with the Viet Cong because they were no longer children; they were now the enemy.

I immediately grabbed one of them, pointed a gun at his head, and told the others to get away from the helicopter; the boy kicked and bit me to try to escape. Still, I put the hammer down on my gun.

I was ready to kill him, but suddenly I heard my mother begging me, "Please, please don't kill him; I didn't give you my life so you could take the life of another mother's child."

I paused and realized I had to listen to my mom before doing something that might scar my soul. So, I unholstered the gun.

I continued to hold the boy with one hand. Still, with the other, I picked up a soccer ball and signaled to the others to invite them to play with me. It took us a while, but then we went back to making one, and I could play with them instead of us all killing each other.

That night, as I flew back to the carrier, I realized that my career as a Marine had ended.

FALSO
ROBERT T. KIYOSAKI

FROM FORGIVENESS TO LOVE

We may think, mistakenly, that the one we are going to forgive should be grateful to us for doing so and render honors. **But remember, forgiveness is a decision and a process whose reward is freedom of the soul.**

To forgive more efficiently, we must stop focusing on the faults of others. We must make an effort and try to see their virtues, no matter how difficult it may be. Forgiving will make you grow as a person, strengthening your values and love.

A prayer is a great tool that helps a lot if we are immersed in the process of forgiving someone.

SIXTEEN

CONDESCENSION

Condescension is a human quality that expresses kindness. It is an attitude that individuals may adopt to please their tastes, preferences, or will. In a negative sense, it can be a feigned kindness that stems from an idea of superiority towards another person. What you will read below will make you reflect on the behavior of human beings.

AND WE SAID OK

In an interview on The Early Show, Jane Clayson asked speaker and author Ana Graham: "How could God let something like this happen?" referring to the September 11 attacks.

Ana Graham gave an incredibly profound and insightful response.

Like us, I believe this event deeply saddens God, but we have been telling Him to get out of our schools, governments, and lives for years.

How can we expect God to give us His blessing and His protection if we demand He leave us alone? I think it all started when Madeleine Murray O'Hare, a well-known promoter of atheism in the United States, complained she didn't want prayer in our schools, and we said OK.

Madeleine was murdered on September 29, 1995, in San Antonio, Texas.

Then, someone said you better not read the Bible in school, even though the Bible says thou shall not kill, thou shall not steal, and love your neighbor as yourself...

And we said OK.

Then Dr. Benjamin Spock said we shouldn't spank our children when they misbehave because their little personalities would be warped, and we might damage their self-esteem.

And we said OK.

We said an expert should know what he's talking about. But Dr. Spock's son committed suicide.

Then, someone said teachers and principals better not discipline our children when they misbehave...

And the school administrators said no faculty member in this school better touch a student when they misbehave because we don't want any bad publicity, and we surely don't want to be sued.

(There is a big difference between disciplining and touching, beating, smacking, humiliating, kicking, etc.)

And we said OK.

Then someone said, let's our daughters have abortions if they want, and they won't even have to tell their parents.

And we said OK.

Then some wise school board member said, since boys will be boys and they're going to do it anyway, let's give our sons all the condoms they want, so they can have all the fun they desire, and we won't have to tell their parents they got them at school.

And we said OK.

Then some of the top elected officials said it doesn't matter what we do in private as long as we do our jobs. And agreeing with them, we said it doesn't matter to me what anyone, including the President, does in private as long as I have a job and the economy is good.

And we said OK.

And then someone else took that appreciation a step further and published pictures of nude children and then stepped further still by making them available on the Internet because they're entitled to their free speech.

Then the entertainment industry said: let's make TV shows and movies that promote profanity, violence, and illicit sex. Let's record music that encourages rape, drugs, murder, suicide, and satanic themes...

And we said OK.

And now we wonder...

Why do our children have no conscience?

Why don't they know the difference between right and wrong?

Why it doesn't bother them to kill strangers, their classmates, and themselves?

Probably, if we think about it long and hard enough, we can figure it out.

"We reap what we sow."

It is curious to see how people go after the negative things in this world to follow a fashion and then wonder why the world's going to hell...

It is curious to see how we believe what the newspapers say, but question what the Bible says...

It is curious why the word of God is suppressed in schools, in the workplace, and sometimes even at home...

SEVENTEEN

HUMAN VALUES

After analyzing and reflecting on the above topic, I felt a burning desire to contribute my grain of sand to the welfare of humanity to reconquer all those human virtues gradually lost.

This situation motivated me to investigate the matter. As a result of this search, I found an audiovisual article in which the Mexican theologian, Pepe González, makes an exposition about **human values**. I decided it would be valuable to share it with you through this writing, so you can make them yours, live by them, and share them with others.

Human values are those positive aspects that allow us to live together with others reasonably to achieve an overall benefit as a society.

There are four groups of human values that lead us to experience a fulfilling life; I will talk about them below.

VITAL OR BIOLOGICAL VALUES

These help us preserve life and lead us towards fullness and maturity. We will describe the scale of importance from a lesser to a greater relevance. We will start with the least important until we reach the most transcendent, because life is about transcending. So, first, we find health, but also nutrition. Some people do not take care of their health and nutrition; they eat pure "junk food," which brings them more or less severe consequences. Hygiene is also included. Bathing every day, brushing your teeth when you get up, after every meal, and at night before going to bed, using deodorant, etc. In addition, you should keep the place where you live clean and tidy; as one of the first Christian thinkers, St. Augustine of Hippo used to say:

"Keep order, and order will keep you."

God wants us healthy, well-fed, and clean. Hygiene is essential, as is looking presentable and self-esteem. A person who does not love himself, does not take care of his health, does not take care of his food or is untidy, does not brush his teeth, has terrible breath, or walks around with dirty hair, demonstrates signs of not appreciating these strong values. And an individual who does not love himself cannot give others something he does not have for himself. To the extent that you value yourself, you will respect others. Now, ask yourself, how are your strong or biological values? These we cannot even call human values since we share them with animals. They also take care of their health and their food. They do not kill for killing; they hunt to survive and manage their hygiene. I have witnessed some quadrupeds grooming their young with licks, and each animal has its way of doing it according to its species. Perhaps you have seen documentaries related to animal life. We can see how they protect their young from predators; then, it is inconceivable to see humans doing the opposite. Some mothers kill their children; individuals kill for money; others kill for pure pleasure. It is unfortunate to think animals, being irrational, could surpass man in terms of behavior.

HUMAN OR CULTURAL VALUES

Human or cultural values are those positive virtues that allow us to coexist in an organized way with other people and enjoy the common welfare as a society. We can find a study, your profession, a postgraduate degree, a doctorate, a master's degree, etc. We can include other intellectual achievements: art, painting, music, learning a language or playing musical instruments, taking a computer, cooking, or driving course, or a workshop that teaches how to manage emotions. All of these can be framed within what cultural values are.

Taking a course to understand the Bible elevates our knowledge. It enlarges our spirit and attending conferences related to these topics or going on a retreat. These are human values that add to our academic formation and our transcendence, which help us grow and not degrade ourselves and encourage the habit of good reading.

If you can, take trips and visit different countries. Traveling allows you to learn without books. You discover cultures, traditions, gastronomy, ways of thinking, and dressing in them. These are enriching and are human or cultural values. That is why we send our children to school or different courses; we want them to grow up having human values; it is part of their formation.

These are just a few examples, but this list of values can continue to grow.

Some people have no culture; they have had the opportunity and have not valued it, don't be one of them.

MORAL VALUES

Moral values are the norms and customs transmitted by society to the individual, representing the suitable and correct way of acting. Allow us to differentiate between good and evil, right and wrong, and unjust.

Parents or authority figures must instill moral values from childhood; teachers or professors must reinforce them.

Many of them are determined by the religion we practice. Others are so deeply rooted in our societies that the violation of one or more of them can lead to legal sanctions.

Examples of moral values are honesty, respect, gratitude, loyalty, tolerance, solidarity, generosity, friendship, kindness, humility, purity, justice, prudence, responsibility, and forgiveness. In short, it isn't easy to list them all.

Specific hierarchical scales among moral values force us to prioritize some over others during a conflict. For example, someone can be a lawyer but corrupt, and what good is that? He can be a doctor, but what good is that without ethics? What good are a lot of cultural values? Suppose he is a liar or a fraud. What good is it to have the walls of an office full of diplomas, postgraduate degrees, and master's degrees if he lives in impurity, stealing, if he is not ethical, or if he does not respect anyone?

You can have a lot of intellectual achievements. Still, if moral values do not support them, they translate into a decadent state at the social level. Moral values make us transcend, but many people are stuck in solid cultural values; they are not ethical. Now ask yourself, how are your biological, human, and moral values?

SPIRITUAL VALUES

Spiritual values are the principles or virtues that can create a close relationship between man and God. They favor their personal growth; these are manifested in each individual's personality and all aspects of his life as a man, husband, head of the household, and worker.

The person who lives according to spiritual values considers the non-material things in his life, giving them more excellent value, knowing that, in the same way, material things. They are of great importance in daily life to find the reason for the situations in human life. In addition, they strengthen faith and reinforce a religious belief, causing the person to move away from the earthly plane and get closer to the divine and supernatural one.

Among the spiritual values that are written in the Old and New Testaments are:

Charity: it is nothing more than a feeling of compassion towards a person, suffering his pain as one's own, living his sorrows and longing for the solution to his problems as if one were living it in the flesh, but the most important thing is trying to help while expecting nothing in return. To be charitable comprises being sensitive to the neighbor and allowing him to solve his problems without expecting thanks or remuneration in return.

What is hope? An optimistic state of mind in which what we desire seems possible. In this sense, hope implies having positive expectations related to that which is favorable, and which corresponds to our desires.

Hope is the opposite of despair. It often serves as a moral pretext for not falling into discouragement, not losing serenity, or abandoning what we long to achieve. Hence, hope positively nourishes our aspirations. In the same way, from an opposing point of view. Hope can be associated with the vein idea of achieving things or realizing our desires, leaving everything to wait and forgetting action, as if we could achieve our objectives without intervening in their realization.

FAITH

What is faith? It is a virtue with which all human beings are endowed, but it is classified into three levels that I will share with you right now. Many people do not know this, so I decided to write about this topic. There are three levels of faith, and they are the following.

Natural or human faith, **theological** or doctrinal faith, **expectant** or working faith.

NATURAL OR HUMAN FAITH

Natural faith is what all human beings who inhabit the earth have, in the different religions, races, and even skeptics. Faith allows us to trust each other, in business, in agreements between peoples, governments, and dignitaries. The newborn child depends on his father and mother; he knows who his father and mother are. It is an attitude that makes us believe and trust each other, but this is not enough; we must advance to the next level of faith.

THEOLOGICAL OR DOCTRINAL FAITH

Theological faith is a genuine faith already formed, an indoctrinated faith; for example, do you believe the Bible is the word of God? It is called theological faith. Do you believe in the sacraments, in Church, in the catechism? That is theological faith; you feed your theological faith when you watch religious programs on TV.

Most of us are in the first two levels, genuine faith, and theological faith, but there is another level of trust; I am referring to expectant faith.

EXPECTANT OR WORKING FAITH

The expectant faith is the one that makes things happen; it translates into works of love and mercy placed at the service of others; it is the belief that God truly exists. He is at our disposal to help us solve daily problems. It is a way to appease our anguish, despair, and worries, since by having faith in God, we humans believe he will help us, filling us with hope.

DEGRADATION OF HUMAN VALUES

The degradation of values is a social phenomenon that stands out today. Some people are looking to achieve their goals, objectives, and successes. For this, they can do anything, even go over other people's heads, cheating, and breaking their ethics and dignity to achieve their purpose.

Nowadays, we can also observe that people think only about themselves; they do not think about others, not even the people closest. They are often not interested in their own family or partner. This degradation of human values has made people highly selfish and only interested in achieving their goals.

Nowadays, women do not need a man. They no longer see him as necessary in their lives, so, many times, they do not get married but live freely without worrying about anyone. They are not tied to the obligation of forming a home to raise children and take care of them. And with men, it has been seen they denigrate women and do not think about the harm they can cause them by deceiving them or playing with their feelings.

Women think only of themselves, and men hurt women's feelings; these two aspects have caused today's relationships not to last. Society is immersed in individualism in which personal satisfaction predominates over the lives of others, not thinking about the community or how to contribute to it, only thinking about winning.

A person who does not cultivate his moral and spiritual values degrades his life and immediately falls into **materialism**, ambition, greed, malice, and the accumulation of material things. That person eventually loses his values, and generosity does not prevail in his life. Materialism leads to **hedonism**. The search for pleasure, practicing the law of minimum effort, and living full of luxuries make the person consumerist and wasteful, and materialism and hedonism lead to **relativism**. We live today have a materialistic, hedonistic, and relativistic culture.

What is relativism? There are no longer absolute truths; everyone has their reality and criteria; nothing is a sin anymore; it is a matter of approach. Some boast and say they have a holistic mind; they are at the forefront, and are advanced, which is sin; for some, it is not. They believe they are free of these things. God does not exist, there is no heaven, and there is no hell; they are inventions of the church, and the sacraments are to manipulate. The Bible is a simple history book. It is not the word of God, and in the Eucharist, there is no Jesus; it is more manipulation of the priests.

To confess to a man who is like any other man, what for? God does not exist, nor the devil, nor the saints. They are pure utopias, pure theories to instill fear and manipulate; everyone can believe what he wants, and everyone has his truth. The commandments, which commandments? You create your reality, your own God, your commandments; let no one tells you what is right or wrong; everything is relative. Relativism takes you to the fourth level of degradation, permissiveness.

PERMISSIVISM

What is permissiveness? It shows flexibility when setting limits or exercising authority. A permissive person shows tolerance towards the transgression of rules or, at least, is open to the exchange of opinions and reasons before deciding.

If a teacher announces the date of an exam and, after pleas from her students, decides to postpone it for a few days, it could be a permissive person.

On the other hand, a parent will be described as permissive when they allow their child to perform certain activities or act in specific ways. Other parents might censure or reprove them. A permissive parent, for example, would allow their adolescent child to roam the streets alone, even at night. Or would enable them to attend rock concerts with their friends or accept that their child's not studying when they do not want to.

PERMISSIVENESS AND ITS CONSEQUENCES

Nowadays, more families are becoming aware of how important it is for their children to develop their future personalities and the style of upbringing they should be guided in life. While it is true to say parents' relationship with their children should be spontaneous. It should not be forgotten that every word, gesture, and lesson parents give to their children during the first years of life is also essential, as it will mark their condition forever.

EIGHTEEN

THE LITTLE ANGELS

We were all happy little angels floating in heaven a long time ago.

God, the omnipotent director, and Savior, watches how men act on earth in heaven.

Desolation reigned; the Father saw so many humans at war, husbands and wives who did not complement each other in spirit, rich and poor apart, healthy, and sick distant, free and enslaved people separated. The Lord sighed, then gathered an army of angels and said to them,

"Can you see the humans? They need help! I need some volunteers to come down and make heaven on earth."

Immediately, all the angels raised their hands and asked, excited and full of faith...

"We?"

"Yes, you are the ones. No one else could fulfill this task. I made man in my image and likeness, but each one with special talents. I allowed for differences among them so that they would form a kingdom together. Some would attain riches to share with the poor. Others would enjoy good health to care for the sick. Some would be wise and others very simple to procure feelings of love, admiration, and respect. The good would have to pray for those who would act as if they were bad. The patient would tolerate the neurotic. In short, my plans must be fulfilled so that man may enjoy, from the earth, eternal happiness. And to achieve this, you will go down with them!"

"What is it all about?" asked the little angels.

"As men have forgotten that I have made you different so you can complement each other and form the body of my beloved son, you will come down with clear distinctions and special tasks to save the world. As angels, you know your mission and your virtues on earth are unions, faith, hope, and charity governed by love; you have known how to forgive. With great patience, you spend your lives illuminating all those who have wanted to love you."

Before saying goodbye to God and the other angels, one of the new human beings raised his hand.

"Why should our mission be so difficult," he asked, "don't all human beings want what we have? Don't they want heaven on earth?"

"Yes, they do," said God, smiling, "but remember, they are angels too."

"Then why is our mission supposed to be so complicated? Why will it be difficult to create a heaven on earth?" the angel insisted.

"Because I gave humans a mind," said God.

"And what's the problem with having a mind?" the angel continued.

"When you have a mind, it takes over, and you forget heaven exists. Your parents will first want to educate your mind to match their way of thinking. They will send you to a church to learn about right and wrong. And then they will send you to school to learn there are smart people and stupid people," the Lord explained.

"So, when we get to earth, our task will be to remember to go beyond our minds, remember we are all angels, and create heaven on earth," asked the angel.

"That's right," said God, smiling. "Humans use the word 'I'; this word comes from the ego and the mind. 'I' represents an illusion; the 'I' completely loses its link with heaven."

The angels heard God's warning about the word "I," and then another one of them asked,

"And what if we forget we are all angels if we fail and cannot build heaven on earth?"

"They will keep dying and being born again and again, until, at last, they remember they are little angels...,"

God explained. "This will be the last time I communicate directly with you," said God. "in a moment, heaven will be erased, and you will receive your mind."

"But how will we talk to you?" asked another angel.

"When you come to earth, you will be taught to pray, and when you pray, you will be speaking, not I."

"How will you talk to us?" asked the angel.

"You will never hear my voice again," said God with a smile. "I will communicate with you through quietness."

"Do you mean silence?"

"No," said God, "quietness is the peace beyond silence. Quietness is perceived when you see a lake early in the morning before the wind stirs the surface. Quietness is the peace you will feel when you look at the sky."

"How will we know you are speaking to us?"

"When your mind is silent, and you feel peace, you will know I am with you; as long as your mind keeps talking, you will not be able to hear me. Mind is very arrogant. It will make you believe you can understand me and be smarter than me; it is extremely arrogant and knows nothing," said God.

"What will we know?" asked another angel.

"You will know that I am with you when you become one with a beautiful sunrise, when you are one with the stars, with a tree, with a flower, with a bubbling brook, when you are one with what is outside of you, you will feel I am there. When you feel peace and your mind is silent, when your soul connects as one with a flower, with the human being in front of you, I will be with you in the present and the now."

"When we become one, we will be with you," asked another angel.

"Yes, as soon as you receive your mind, you will become two; you will be separated from all my creatures and creations. Your mind will begin to catalog, criticize, judge, and pretend to be God."

"How can we connect with you?" the angel continued.

"Through the peace that links with my other creations. You can also pray. I will be there when you connect your inner beauty with your outer beauty in quietness and meditation," God explained.

"When we pray, we will talk to you, but for you to talk to us, do we have to turn off our minds, be quiet and pray?" asked the angel.

"Yes, but you will not listen to anything I say," said God.

"What will happen if we practice calmness and meditation and remain in the now?" asked another angel.

"They will be more and more united with me. One day you will see a flower from your soul, not from your thought, and you will exclaim, 'Oh, my God,' then I will be with you," explained God.

"And will you be the one to speak to us?" continued the angel, and God nodded?

"Now go, you will remember none of this, but when you feel the peace and wonder of 'Oh, my God!' in your soul more and more each day, we will be together, for you will remember you are little angels and working with me to build heaven on earth."

"And will there comes a day when we will live forever in that glorious moment when we say 'Oh, my God!?"

God nodded again.

"But we don't have to be little angels on earth, do we?" asked another angel.

"No," said God, "that is why we will give them a mind divided in two and fed by the ego. You will be human beings; you will always have the freedom to choose which side of your mind you want to be on. Do not forget everything on earth is a duality; you will find good and evil, matter and spirit, realism, and idealism, rich and poor. Your challenge as humans will be to become 'one with life' again, connect with everything, and rejoin."

The time to leave came, and God gave each little angel a gift in beautiful wrapping.

"Here is your mind; each is different, which means you will all be human, but not the same. The challenge will be to learn to be with each other, bond in spirit, and love each other despite your differences."

One of the little angels asked,

"How long will we live without seeing you?"

Another questioned:

"How long will we be away from you?"

"Don't worry; I will be with you every day. Besides, this will only last a few years; it will only be an instant on the eternal clock," said the Lord.

The angels accepted their beautiful gifts. And God said to them:

"Go now."

As soon as they took the gifts, their beautiful memories of heaven were erased.

God chose several and then prepared them for the birth process.

The angels were happy with the Lord's choice, although it caused them great sadness to leave heaven to fulfill their mission.

Finally, they wished them "good luck."

And they came down to earth excited.

They were assigned parents and the country where they would be born.

Each one arrived in a mother's womb, where they were formed for nine months.

Some parents refused the task; others took it on angrily; others blamed each other until their marriage dissolved. Still, others wept with love and accepted the duty.

NINETEEN

THE HEALING POWER OF DOING GOOD

Research shows that helping others brings peace of mind that lasts long after the kind act has been performed.

Brain studies show that assisting others brings us a deep state of joy and delight from cultivating generosity.

HOW TO HELP?

Solving, helping, and serving are acts of charity in different ways; the most important thing is to accept people in whatever situation they are in.

Sometimes, it is difficult to be generous because we do not know what to do or say when someone is in distress, pain, or discomfort.

The key is listening and knowing that your presence will speak very well of you.

How can I help? It has become very significant for many people in recent years. However, the real question would be, how can I be of service? There are times when you can solve a difficult situation for some people.

For example, you can donate part of your family's food or clothes to people affected by a natural disaster. You can help a convalescent older adult with shopping and basic activities. If you own a restaurant, you can make sandwiches and give them to the poor or homeless people in your area; you can also help by picking up trash in parks or planting trees.

It is essential to look around your neighborhood and look for immediate needs.

SPIRITUAL BENEFITS OF HELPING OTHERS

Some studies show that helping others decreases colds, increases joy, self-esteem, stress, and even less physical pain.

After reading this section, you have probably discovered that being kind and charitable to others is beneficial to both you and the recipient.

Other research shows the happier you live, the more optimistic you are about your actions.

Happiness, it seems, stimulates the desire to make the world a better place.

True happiness cannot exist while others suffer; it comes only from serving others and living in harmony with nature.

If you are financially solvent, an excellent way to use your money is to contribute to charitable causes to better this world.

No matter how much or how little you can give, the needy will always thank you for the gesture.

The gestures of gratitude and the smiles you receive from those you help are valuable gifts that nourish the soul more than the material things the world offers us.

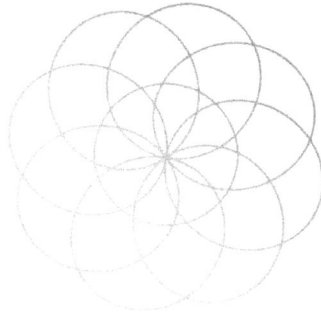

CONCLUSION

Throughout this paper, we have reflected on how we have to develop our generosity by offering and sharing our time with others. We have also seen how being charitable is a choice we must make voluntarily to contribute to the world around us and express our generosity.

A primary conclusion is when we have blossomed as humans, we find our path and life of progress, which will bring us fulfillment. It is certainly not challenging to flourish if we are willing to grow and develop our values.

After having shared this work with you, let me ask you two questions:

1- What values will you put into practice by serving others in the next three days?

2- With what act of kindness and gentleness could you make a difference? You can start now.

God has granted a precious life to each of us. Every day, upon awakening, our first thought should be how fortunate we are to have awakened one more day and that we are alive to contemplate the beauty of Divine Creation in its fullness.

Remember to lead a life of spiritual growth and always prosper.

The dawn is the most beautiful part of the day because it is when God tells you to get up! He gives you another opportunity to live and start holding His hand again.

In this book, we saw how to develop:

- Self-esteem
- Cordiality
- Gratitude
- Forgiveness
- Empathy
- The healing power of doing good

- It will help you find heaven on earth

Human blossoming is the set of values a person has and shares with others by professing true love; by his acts of kindness, he achieves a prosperous and fulfilling life.

By reading this book, you probably learned to have mental flexibility, improve your interpersonal relationships, and be tolerant and objective; indeed, your presence is pleasant, which is why others feel good by your side.

I want to dedicate a few words to thank you for taking the time to read this book. I have written with a lot of passion for sharing my knowledge and my experience of human blossoming with you.

"Good days give you HAPPINESS,
bad days give you EXPERIENCE,
attempts to keep you STRONG,
trials keep you, HUMAN
the falls keep you HUMBLE,
but only God keeps you STANDING."

SAINT JOHN PAUL II

DESCRIPTION OF THE EMBLEM

The white flower is the *cymbidium* orchid, representing virtues, morals—values and respect for others. White symbolizes purity, enlightenment, and innocence.

The five petals represent the number five: spiritual growth, balance, and equilibrium in our lives.

The sun is the light that invites us to see hidden truths, wisdom, and enlightenment through cultivating knowledge and spiritual awareness.

Orange/gold represents energy, happiness, human warmth, and anointing.

The heart represents the feeling of love and devotion to oneself and others. Crimson red/brown represents strength, power, and creativity.

The open hands represent sharing our good fortune with those in need.

In the image's background, the spiral or seed of life represents the divine plan, the interconnection between life as vibrational energy and creation. The outward expansion from the divine source. Action and movement.

In summary:

"The purity found in the virtues is illuminated by spiritual awareness and unconditional love; these must be shared with others as a part of the divine plan that is still active."

BIBLIOGRAPHY

Kiyosaki, R. T. (2019). Fake. (1st. Ed). Mexico City.

Penguin Random House Grupo Editorial, S. A. de C.V: 533 pp.

Lozano, C. (2017). A Positive Attitude. (1st. Ed) Miami, Fl33156.

Penguin Random House Grupo Editorial, S. A. de C.V: 250 pp.

Osteen, J. (2007). Become a Better You. (1st. Ed.) New York, NY.

10020 free pres. A division of Saimon Schuster, Inc. 377 pp.

The Holy Bible. (1994) 21st Century King James Version (KJ21). (Updating of the 1611 King

James Version). Deuel Enterprises, Inc., Gary, SD 57237.

Chapman, G. (2015) The 5 Love Languages. (1st. Ed.) Northfield Publishing.

Colombia Ediciones Unilit: 191 pp.

Hicks, E. & Hicks, J. (2009) The Vortex: Where the Law of Attraction Assembles All Cooperative Relationships (1st. Ed.) Hay House Inc., California. 284 pp.

Elliot, L. (2017) Tu Libro, Tu Legado. Independently published. 62 pp.

Frank, L, & Victor, E. (1997). Man's Search for Meaning. Simon & Schuster.

SOURCE OF INFORMATION FOR THE REFLECTIONS

- https://sites.google.com/site/elespanolazo/textos/cuentos-y-poemas/cuentos-y-cuentitos/el-billete-arrugado
The Crumpled Bill, (El Billete Arrugado)

- https://www.elclubdeloslibrosperdidos.org
The Beauty of the Greeting (La Belleza del Saludo)

- https://marianoosorio.com/blogs/reflexiones/los-angelitos
The Little Angels (Los Angelitos). Mariano Osorio (Adapted by Arles Ballesteros)

- https://tucuentofavorito.com/la-ventana-del-hospital-cuento-corto-sobre-la-empatia/
The Hospital Window (La Ventana del Hospital)

- https://renuevo.com/power-point-imposible-atravesar-la-vida.html
  Impossible to Go Through Life (Imposible atravesar la vida)

- https://educacionparalasolidaridad.com/2017/02/01/una-historia-real-del-joven-llamado-albert-einstein/
  True Story of the Man Named Albert Einstein (Historia real del hombre llamado Albert Einstein)

- https://marianoosorio.com/blogs/reflexiones/estoy-harto-de-la-vida
  I'm Sick of Life (Estoy harto de la vida)

- https://www.reflexionesparaelalma.net/page/reflexiones/id/169/title/Y-Dijimos-que-estaba-Bien...
  And We Said OK (Y dijimos que estaba bien)

- https://reflexionesdiarias.wordpress.com/2007/12/19/de-todos-modos/
  Anyways (De todos modos)

- https://docer.com.ar/doc/88c1x1
  There are no Atheists in the Trenches (En las trincheras no hay ateos) From the book "Fake" by Robert Kiyosaki, chapter 13, title: "A student of God," pp. 314. 1ra. Edicion esp. Sept. 2019. (Adapted by Arles Ballesteros)

"I hope the end of this book marks the beginning of a new chapter in your life."

Arles Ballesteros - Author.

RECOMMENDED TEXTS FOR FURTHER READING

In this book, Blossoming Through Virtues, I recommend some self-help works that will motivate you to have thoughts of kindness and desires to help others.

I will list some texts from which I was inspired to write this book; I invite you to read them so you can develop the virtues that will help you lead a life of blossoming.

I hope that the end of this book will be the beginning of a new phase in your life.

THERE IS A BOOK INSIDE OF YOU (HAY UN LIBRO DENTRO DE TI) - Raimón Samsó

YOUR BOOK, YOUR LEGACY (TU LIBRO, TU LEGADO) - Dr. Laura Elliot

FAKE (FALSO) - Robert T. Kiyosaki

REFLECTION THE LITTLE ANGELS (LOS ANGELITOS)—Mariano Osorio

AUTHOR BIOGRAPHY

Arles Omar Ballesteros Fernández is a person of good faith and with good moral principles. He promotes the value of love and enjoys sharing his knowledge of personal development and self-improvement with others.

He was born into a humble family in Olanchito, the civic city of Honduras, on September 2, 1966. At the age of seventeen, he migrated to another city, inspired by a spirit of self-improvement, dedicating himself to various chores and work to support himself and help his parents. He worked on creating metal structures and crafts as a welder, washing dishes, waiter, and furniture maker, and was a sailor for several years. He did all of this while finishing his high school education at nights, yet he still achieved his graduation with honors.

Art is also an essential part of his life. Apart from writing and being an avid reader, he also enjoys making origami; even though he is left-handed, he plays the guitar and piano very well, composes songs, and sings. He also creates ornamental metal sculptures.

Today, he lives in the United States with his wife and three children and wishes to share with the world what he believes, based on his experiences, is the true purpose of man's existence on earth and some secrets and techniques to be genuinely authentic happy.

I ASK FOR YOUR SUPPORT

Please help me make this book reach more people. Leave your honest **review or comment** on Amazon or any other digital platform where you purchased it. I have to rely on the readers for the success of this book.

COMMENTS

For comments: arlesballestero666@gmail.com

Facebook: Arles Ballesteros
Instagram: @Arles.Ballesteros

For more information about the book or the author, scan this QR Code

https://quisqueyanapress.com/arles-ballesteros

www.ingramcontent.com/pod-product-compliance
Lightning Source LLC
Chambersburg PA
CBHW032056020426
42335CB00011B/366